Nineteen
Fifty-Seven

COTEAU BOOKS

www.coteaubooks.com

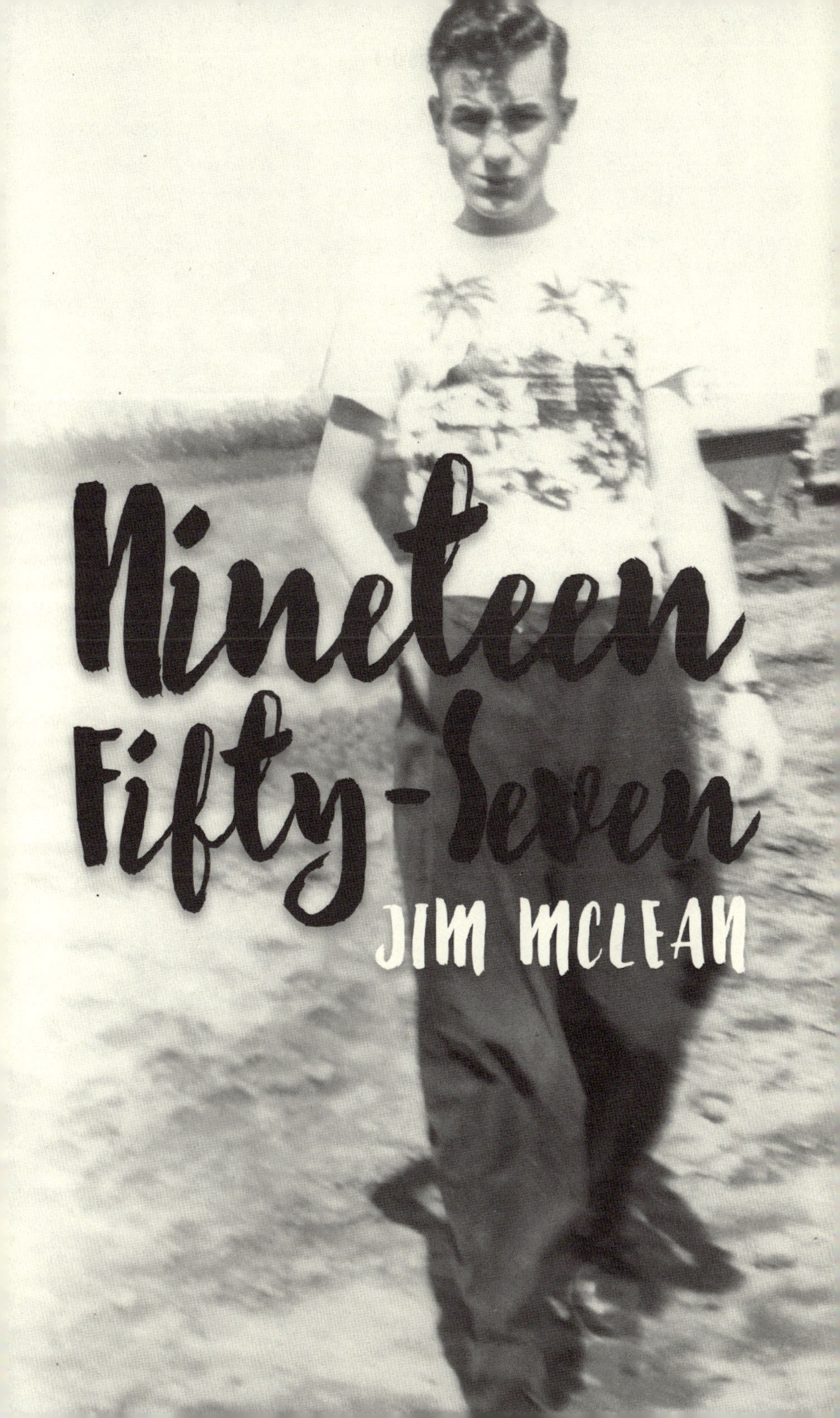

Nineteen Fifty-Seven

JIM MCLEAN

Edited by Harold Rhenisch
Cover design by Jamie Olson
Typeset by Susan Buck
Printed and bound in Canada

Library and Archives Canada Cataloguing in Publication

McLean, Jim, 1940-, author
Nineteen fifty-seven / Jim McLean.

Issued in print and electronic formats.

ISBN 978-1-55050-675-4 (paperback).--ISBN 978-1-55050-676-1 (pdf)

I. Title. II. Title: 1957.

PS8625.C538N56 2016 C811'.6 C2016-903557-3
C2016-903558-1

COTEAU BOOKS

2517 Victoria Avenue
Regina, Saskatchewan
Canada S4P 0T2
www.coteaubooks.com

Available in Canada from:
Publishers Group Canada
2440 Viking Way
Richmond, British Columbia
Canada V6V 1N2

10 9 8 7 6 5 4 3 2 1

Coteau Books gratefully acknowledges the financial support of its publishing program by: the Saskatchewan Arts Board, The Canada Council for the Arts, the Government of Saskatchewan through Creative Saskatchewan, the City of Regina. We further acknowledge the [financial] support of the Government of Canada. Nous reconnaissons l'appui [financier] du gouvernement du Canada.

Saskatchewan Arts Board · Canada Council for the Arts / Conseil des Arts du Canada · Canada · Government of Saskatchewan

To the memory of my friend Bing Trew,
present in many of these poems.

Table of Contents

Work

Dark World

Memories

Writing

Writing

Music

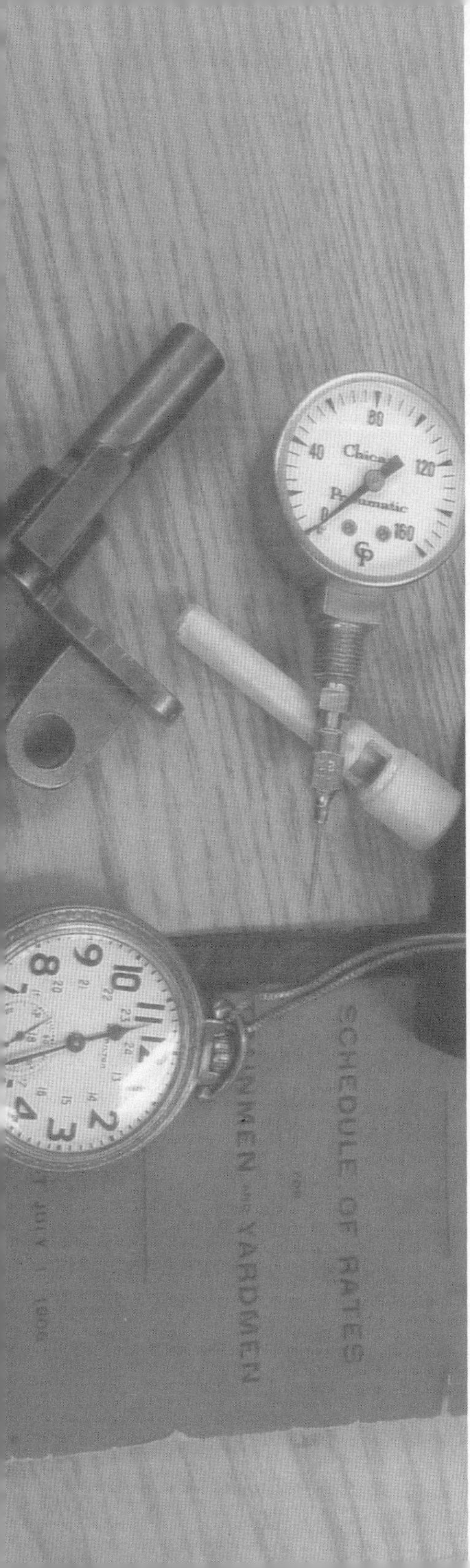

Work

Comet West

this poem
is a way to remember

those nights
in C Yard or D Yard or F Yard

tying hoses in the darkness
laying my lamp on the ties

left foot always outside the rail
in case the slack ran in

springing to safety whenever
the switch crew would throw

a block into the next track
not even embarrassed anymore

jumping like that
it happening so often

night after night   alone
in that unbelievable silence

under the stars debating
great philosophical questions

with myself, taking one side
then the other   or a third

not boring anyone
no one listening but me

walking the train with the air
after the engines tied on

changing the odd gasket
careful when reaching

over the drawbars to turn
the angle cock   always alert

for movement   sometimes a trainman
would volunteer to get the hoses

on a double-over but I always rode down
in case he forgot to cut the air in

or flubbed a hose   some guys would get
offended but it was my job and anyways

it was good to walk the cars, listen for leaks
watch for handbrakes   the year

of the big comet up there every night
never seeming to move

About MacKay

they never ran a television program
about that Sunday morning

MacKay stuck the 12-gauge in his mouth
and sprayed his brains

all over the walls of that railway bunk car
wasn't even his gun

it belonged to the welding gang foreman
he did it on the foreman's bed

his last raucous joke
the foreman was a rough old bugger

said he'd have killed MacKay
if he wasn't already dead

no CBC reporters asking how it was
he came to be this hopeless alcoholic

or how he might have been queer
back when being that way

was the worst thing a man could be
he never tried anything, not with me anyway

maybe he didn't know himself
probably suspected it though

at least he had the guts to do it
I mean killing himself

instead of talking shit
like this asshole on the CBC

whining about all the times
he had the rope around his neck

times he wanted to O.D. or jump
off a building going on and on

to some intense forward-leaning
personality conscious of her own

profile in the camera lights
wringing her hands

like he was some kind of shining
downtrodden victim of society

so maybe she can get one of them
countless fucking awards

they hand out, hell all I remember
about MacKay was him laughing

and ordering another round and
shooting himself that Sunday.

After

all those years, the calls in the night, somebody ran through a
switch and
sideswiped a half-dozen cars, round the clock at wrecks in winter
or in the sweat of
summer or called to the picket line and what the hell is this bull-
shit, pulling night duty
every time, where are those bastards who showed up drunk at the
meetings with all that
workers of the world unite crap but don't show up for picket
duty, let somebody else do it
or later on, in management, fighting the picket lines, trying to get
those from other trades
with contracts in to honour their obligations, Christ, night after
night and those bastards
from the CN showing up after their afternoon shift to cause
trouble.

but good times too, out in the summer on the Glenboro sub the
Manitoba sunset lasting
forever, the land down there as flat as a billiard table, top-soil so
deep the farmers still
burned their stubble, the wind fouling our ballast with that rich
black earth. We'd pull
grain trains up that line with all the tonnage we had power for
and we started running trains of empties out of Winnipeg in late
afternoon to spot the elevators at night. The crews didn't like it,
they had to lay-over at Souris and work both directions in the
dark but it just made sense to spot empties for morning loading
and lift the loads after the elevator men had gone home

and riding down to Altona on the coveted work assignment, the
whole town smelling of linseed oil from the crushing plant and
Percy the Roadmaster's standing joke about the two towns on the
Emerson sub. *Otterbourne. Niverville!*

one time, Jimmy Babson and I were checking operations on the Rail Change-Out Gang near Regina. Naturally, we were wearing boots and blue jeans and at noon we drove to the Saskatchewan Hotel for lunch. The waiter looked at us and told us the dining-room was full, we could see it wasn't but he herded us into a side room. I said we could go somewhere else but Jimmy said no, let's stay. The waiter gave us the same menu they were using for the civilized people. The next day, we went back in suits and ties. The same guy led us to a table but Jimmy pointed to the side room, said, we'll sit in there. The waiter said, oh, no, I'll sit you in the main dining room. Poor guy, it wasn't his fault, but we made him squirm.

that winter up near Leader, long before the safety rules, pulling tanks of butane with steel cables and nothing bad happening which is why I'm still here and there's not one man working the railway today knows about pulling dope or galena or the big ice-houses that used to dominate the skyline just west of the subway or the switch-tender in his shack or the phones where everyone could listen in when someone cranked three short or long short long or whatever or thawing steam lines on the passenger trains at forty below or the morning we were filling Perrier bottles from the Dominion dining-car with a dirty greasy hose when the switch crew pulled a cut of cars away and the diners looked out and watched with their mouths hanging open

or walking those 140-car trains in the dead of winter with our off-set stillsons trying to cut down the air leaks enough to get the trains out and always having to reduce the number of cars by ten or twenty or fifty, depending on the temperature and those god-damned Wabco brakes, the pots frozen up, full of ice, that's all we did that winter, laid under those cars and changed pots

and the poor old hard-luck guy in Winnipeg who got hit by an automobile and was in the hospital full of tubes but wanted to go home he lived in the North End and got somebody's coat and shoes and tried to walk home and got half-way across the yards to where the tail-end cut of 973 was sitting, they always pulled

973 across the South Hump in two cuts and the old guy was crawling under a container flat when they tied on and pulled cut him in three pieces the coroner showed up in a tuxedo and white scarf, he was at a party and I was writing my report at four in the morning on that one

and the time Nick Kurolchuk hit Alex Payson on the shoulder with a packing iron because Alex called him a bohunk and Nick said you son-of-a-bitch I know your family I know you changed your name and guys used to do that all right to get a promotion and I remember we used to lock Jack Sheward, the coach foreman, in a baggage car every night when the passenger train came in because he was always drunk and the night somebody crawled between the crisp white sheets of the General Manager's bed in his private car, crawled in with his overalls and greasy boots. They never caught the guy but we guessed who it was, there was always something happening

and that blizzard when the switch crew was sitting in the shack and Johnny Buxton the hogger was bitching because they had to call a sectionman to sweep the switches and it was taking him so long to get there and I said that poor old bugger worked all day in this and now they call him out at night to sweep switches for you guys, I said, once he sweeps the switch he lines it to make sure it turns so he's already done the yardman's job as well as his own they should give him 15 minutes of training and let him run the fucking engine as well and John didn't like it but he shut his mouth because he knew it was the truth

and all these things coming back at me now how great it was when we got the new auxiliary cars and we could be out there on a wreck and actually be able to shower I remember saying to the Regional Mechanical Officer it was like having an extra crew a man could get clean and sleep properly

I started out labouring on the Rip and we moved those big steel wheels with blocks and suitcases and the dolly, just a big lever, really, about the same as the ancient Greeks and Egyptians used and once you caught on to it you could catch those wheels and spin them around like child's play and then I signed up for an apprenticeship and my wage dropped down to a dollar and three cents an hour, I was indentured I had to stay for five years if I ran away legally they could track me down and bring me back but that probably wouldn't happen and anyway I had a day job for five years with a pay raise every six months as long as I had my math assignments in and working on Wilbur's wheel gang five trucks in the morning, four in the afternoon wheeling the air jacks and lugging the A-frame to the spaces left between the cars or using the car mover to make space or on light repairs putting up draft gears and yokes or the old draft couplers and my knees going from kneeling down on the gravel and concrete all those winters

and just in time getting a promotion and moving upstairs, Tom Farmer the General Car Foreman, he was retired then, coming down to Coffee Row and he was so damned proud of me I felt really good about that what with all the trouble I'd made for him over the years and then DJM coming to town and a whole new era of railroading and moving to Winnipeg with him when he left and all the changes we made there in the winter it was as cold as the bloody moon but it was a great place to railroad and I went over to Operating in '88 and at first I had the branches and then the Main Line and finally had the Yard and working everything – dark territory and MBS and CTC

and getting off the plane at Pearson Airport on August 31, it seemed the whole world was there, everyone coming back to Toronto after the summer and that Rule 292 violation on my desk the first morning what with the new territory and the DOB and the Speed Signals that we didn't use in the West and later were incorporated into the CROR I had my hands full but we did okay and even saved the hogger's job, breaking him to Yard Foreman instead of dismissing him and he was real happy with that, he'd been way out of his depth and moving down to Union Station into Labour Relations and having to learn all those collective agreements, so many trips to Montreal, Mauricio the night desk clerk at the Chateau Champlain welcoming me by name every time I arrived, that always made an impression with any stewardesses checking in at the same time and all those years ago standing on a box car in black lonely F Yard under a universe of stars waving a sputtering fusee for the set-up and after all that and so much more I probably don't remember I find myself wishing I was back there in 1956 on that bright morning in May after the snowfall the night before just starting out because it's the journey, after all

that *aurora borealis*, southern Saskatchewan, summer, and us riding the deck of a flat-car on point, the big hook rattling along behind, running down to the wreck with a monstrous black thunder-storm gathering, thick bolts of lightning seconds in front of the booming thunder, a phenomenon filling the skies – from horizon to the heavens green snakes of undulating light in afternoon darkness and that lightning! the steel rails grounded in the ballast beneath us it was a time to be nervous, to be reasonably afraid but I felt wild. I felt wild riding there on that flat-car, the siding switch coming up and the cold rain beginning to fall.

The Complete History of Radio in Moose Jaw

All the neighbourhood boys
were trained to sprint up the block
knocking at every door, warning people
the radio license inspector was coming
and the people would hurry to pull
electrical plugs from the walls
or hide their big, heavy battery radios
before he made it to their doors.

We were radio license terrorists, devastating
to the inspector's quota. The licenses
were only two dollars or maybe four dollars
but the inspector never collected enough
to justify his existence and he went
the way of the truant officer.

Radio ran like a thread through the community.
We could get CKCK 620 Regina or CBC Watrous
to hear the official time signal at noon
but just about everyone tuned to CHAB
for the weather and the early morning patter
which included the hospital report: *Mabel Jones*
spent a restless night, Nick Moschuk recovering
from surgery, Annie Chalmers receiving visitors.

Sunday mornings there would be a religious service
from a different church each week, followed by
the Sunday Shut-In Program which played requests
from those confined to bed. Sunday was always dreary,
even on the radio, except for Cuckoo Clock House
which came on in the afternoon from CBC Toronto.
I can still sing the opening and closing jingle to that show.

For real small-town corny community mix,
you couldn't beat The Mail Bag. Cy Knight ran that show
like his personal fiefdom and people would write letters
requesting songs or offering eggs or chickens for sale

or announcing the engagements of their daughters
and Cy would play their requests and read their letters,
letters from every town in southern Saskatchewan
as well as from Moose Jaw, with complete equality.

Cy ran a sort of talent show as well, encouraging
local yokels to perform. Some were pretty good and some,
of course, were dreadful. Manley Seeds was a regular
with his one-string guitar.
What are you going to sing for us today, Manley?
The Wreck of the Old '97, Cy.
Gee, Manley, I thought you wrecked that yesterday.
Poor old Manley never caught on, but he was good entertainment.

At night, you could get right up close, no lights,
except for the soft green or red glow from the radio
and listen to Wayne and Schuster, Fibber McGee and Molly,
Our Miss Brooks and Amos 'n Andy and when it got real late,
past time when we should have been in bed, Big Town,
sponsored by Lifebuoy, The Green Lantern, Boston Blackie,
Enemy to Those Who Make Him an Enemy,
Friends to Those Who Have No Friends,
Lux Radio Theatre and the spooky
Murder at Midnight.

Saturday night there was the Hit Parade, two Hit Parades, really,
first the Western Hit Parade, *Saddle Your Troubles to a*
Cowboy Song and Yodel Your Troubles Away, followed by the
Popular Hit Parade. Each one started at Number Ten on the list
and played them right up to Number One, as compiled by
Assiniboia Music at the bottom of Main Street.

There's more, of course, but that would mean taking you through
all those inane soap operas our mothers listened to while baking
or ironing or washing floors or mending and sweeping
as they thrilled to Pepper Young's Family or Ma Perkins.
It would mean dredging up the noon-hour farm report

with its reams of statistics where everything seemed to be listed
at 12 and-a-half cents, cattle prices, canners and cutters,
the hog futures and all that wheat, oats and barley and,
after supper, but before the dishes were done,
Back to the Bible, the program that made all of us happy
to run outside and play.

The Complete History of Milk in Moose Jaw

I started out the same as everybody else,
stealing money from milk bottles.
If there was no money in the empties
the milkman would usually leave the milk
and square up at week's end. Everybody
was honest back then. Of course,
you didn't steal from the same house
every morning, sometimes two days in a row
but never more and you spaced it out
over a few blocks. People grumbled like hell
about paying up twice but the milkman's creased
and soiled notebook had the final say.

The loudmouths would stand around
on the front porches in their undershirts after supper
threatening stake-outs and vigilante action
but who's going to lay in the weeds until four in the morning
over a couple of bottles of milk?
When they came up with tokens
we'd steal the tokens and sell them to the milkman
who'd sell them back to his customers.
It didn't take long for him to wise up
and start stealing the tokens himself.
What goes around comes around.

There used to be three dairies in this town:
Johnstone's, Palm Dairies, and the Co-op.
We got our milk from Johnstone's.
Duff Milligan would let me ride a few
blocks in his horse-drawn wagon,
would let me flick the reins over Old Dolly's back,
her turds trailing behind, sparrows lighting,
picking out the oats. Now, all the milk
comes from Ontario or Quebec
in cardboard cartons or those plastic jugs –
no milkman at the door. Supply management, they call it.

Duff Milligan was the typical milkman
and he had his regular stops. God knows how many
pounds of butter he must have handed over.
At a couple of places, he didn't even bother to record
how many bottles of milk and cream he took in.
I don't know what he was thinking; that horse and wagon
was like a big red flag out on the street.
He had nerve, though, I'll give him that.
It was still a standing joke years later when I was working
on the railway that a man was wise to check
the street in front of his house when he got home from work
to see how high a pile of horseshit was there.

I was riding with Duff once when he stopped at a house,
I won't say where. He told me to stay
with the horse. He said, "If you see a man coming
down the street, come running and pound on the door quick."
Well, he'd been in there a while when I saw the mailman
coming, so I ran to the door and banged
on it like he said to do. Just as the mailman got to the door,
Duff came running out holding up his pants,
knocked the poor guy ass over tea kettle,
mail flying everywhere. Duff gave me a clip
behind the ear. "Goddammit, I said
if you see a man coming, not the mailman!"
I never got to ride with him again.

Just about everyone on the route would give the milkman
a drink at Christmas and if it wasn't for the horse he never
would have gotten back to the dairy.
There were regular fires at the stables
all the time, the hay or the straw igniting
from spontaneous combustion, threatening to burn
down the rickety sheds, horses and all.
Most of the time you could get free buttermilk
at the dairy to feed to the dogs if you brought

your own container and if you asked the milkman
on a hot July day you could always
get a piece of ice to suck and, on really rare occasions,
a bottle of chocolate milk, as long as you smashed
the empty bottle and gave him back the broken neck.

The Moose Jaw Barber's Code

I don't remember any barber changing his style
when he talked to different guys

anymore than he changed the style of the haircuts
buzz, duck-tail, leave the side-burns, long in the back

Maybe that was because the barber always did
most of the talking; you kept your mouth shut

and blew the hair off your lips and just said Mmm-mmm
at appropriate moments. This was always a small

city so there wasn't much of a class system. I remember
this guy he was the city works manager or something

rushing back into the barber's after I'd just settled
in the chair. He was all wound up because he said

the barber had made one ear look lower than the other
Jake asked me if I'd mind and he put the guy back

in the chair and fiddled and diddled a bit and
told him he was good to go. I would have told the guy

his ear looked lower because he was born that way
because one ear was

an inch lower than the other but
a barber had to be diplomatic

Heartbreak Hotel

R. Smith & Sons contracted for the railway,
feeding the gangs of men who came each spring

from the unemployment lines and the jails
and the reserves and the soup kitchens and River Street

to lay steel in the raw early mornings with their pitiable
shabby suit coats and soft, mushy shoes,

a few with caps.
The foremen were tough and seasoned and had to be,

it was still, back then, a long journey
from Moose Jaw to Chaplin. Old Jim,

the cook, was ex-army, 77 years old, his muscle
turned soft, turned to fat, he used to say with regret.

Up at five every morning, first thing he taught me
was not to lean my elbows on the wash stand

when I scrubbed my face in the early dawn.
It was a military thing, I guess, and he would grunt

with satisfaction to see me bend at the waist,
elbows up, over the enameled basin.

It was easy for me to give him that.
He was a pretty good old guy, Polish,

he said he was. He watched, let you show him
what you were made of.

Bill was just about as old as the cook,
skinny as a rail, with a wife at home.

No business being there,
except he needed the money, I guess.

We'd peel potatoes together every morning
for the noon meal and again in the afternoon

to get ready for supper, and talk a bit.
We'd eat our meal after the men

had gone back to the track
or to their bunks at the end of the working day

and Bill would always eat too much,
as if he was trying to store it up,

yet he never put on any weight, he'd just
get sick and then be sorry.

Bill treated me all right
and I liked him but I never wanted

to get that old and be that poor. It was 1956
and I was a kid and on my own out there.

The cook liked the way I could carry whole sides
of beef, his own strength gone,

and he gave me lots of other things to do
but my main job was to wash dishes

I washed those dishes from the meals of those hundred
or more men three times a day

with water hauled from the tender and heated
boiling hot on the stove and I sang

alone, away from everybody, at the top of my lungs
with my hands in the soapy water up to my elbows

every song I knew, Hank Snow and Williams
The Platters and Webb Pierce and I can't remember them all

and, of course, *Heartbreak Hotel*, by that new guy,
that I played every day on the juke-box

in the Chaplin Café beside the tracks when I bought a Coke
and sat on a stool like teen-agers you would see

on television and learned all the words for singing later
away from everybody

River Street

We'd haul empties collected from the ditches
along the highway to the Bottle Exchange Saturday mornings

collecting our twenty cents a dozen, always crossing the street
on our way back to Main, not wanting to pass the doorway

of the Rex Rooms, butt of our smutty jokes,
repository of our juvenile fantasies. We never saw

anyone come or go there but the place held us
like scenes in films *noir*, our induction into dark culture.

All the rough hotels were there on River Street, the Cecil,
Empress, Brunswick, the Kings, later named the Royal

with their vile, dirty, noisy beer parlours, spittoons overflowing
onto the rotted floors, places where women couldn't go, where

wives would telephone, asking for their husbands, the men
waving their hands, *no*, when the barkeep called their names.

Afterwards the men would stumble into The Bamboo
where young hookers sat provocatively at counter stools.

A strange place, River Street, where the genteel people said
no decent God-fearing citizen would go after dark

but the same street where anyone could go in daylight
to Ross Thatcher's Moose Jaw Hardware

or to Sol's Second Hand Store. There were stories
about the vicious bastards down there who'd put

a knife in you just for looking good. I saw torn shirts
and bloody noses but I never saw a knife.

Bill Fredrickson lived in a room over Richard's Inn,
just off Main. Bill drank beer and when he sat down

he'd order ten glasses. He'd order ten for you as well.
Bill was a serious drinker.

Usually, by the time you had a glass or two the rest were gone.
Bill only had a thumb and one finger on his right hand

but he could circle that glass and down it
hardly seeming to swallow. He drank. You bought.

I only went down to River Street with my brother-in-law
because he was a good pool player and he was tough.

If you won at pool down there, if you took their money,
you had to be tough. I think

all that talk about Al Capone hiding out on River Street
was bullshit. Those stories generated some sensational

notoriety but we didn't need it. We had enough
crooked politicians and police chiefs of our own

and, it's a bit sad that, like one of Wittgenstein's headaches
River Street exists now only in this failing memory

or in yours, and only in a few scrawled lines
of poetry, and only until we're gone.

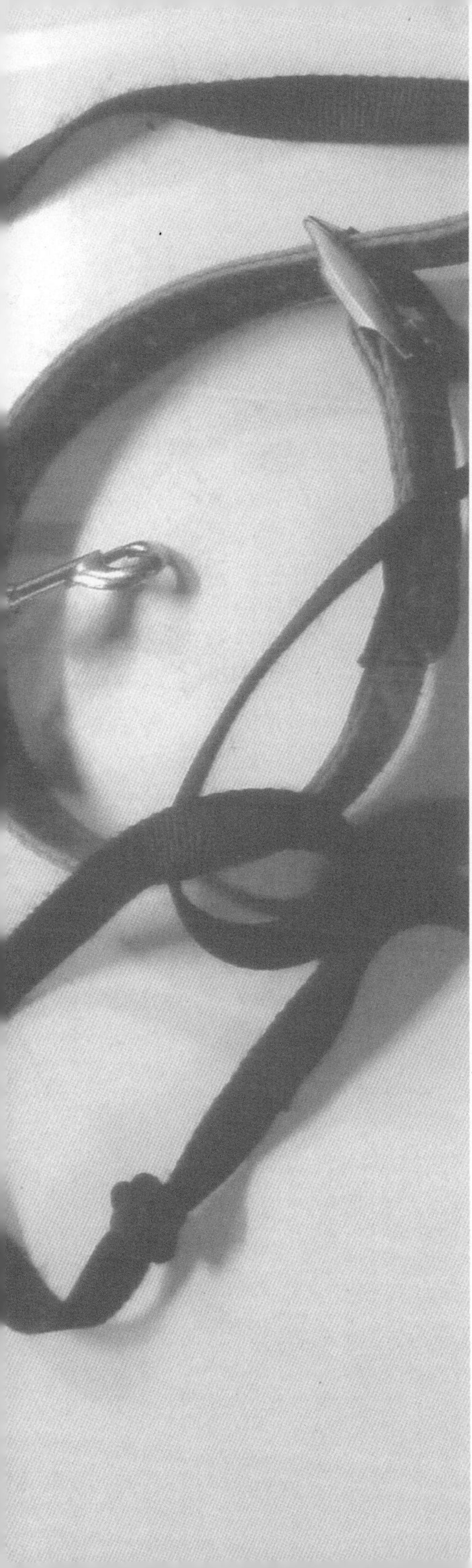

Dark World

Doctor my Eyes

what do you see what do you see right now do you see me
you see me right now I don't see me what if you saw you
right now would you think you were looking in a mirror
or would you think you were looking at yourself
would you think you were crazy?

I see what I see you say oh if everyone saw what you see
you wouldn't be crazy right now I don't see what you see
you don't see what I see are we both crazy or none?
the voices you mean the voices you don't hear I had a
dog whistle and no one could hear it but the dog came

the voices are magnetic like
Hitler what about those crowds of people lining the streets
the women in ecstasy can you sit there and tell me he didn't
enter them his thoughts went into them it's biological really
if you think about it they transmit

their voices along the water pipes in the electrical
wires do you have any idea how many thousands of miles
of pipe and wire there are in the world you can't get away
I remember them calling me when I was a boy walking
to Ross School empty lots and the fields beyond

I could hear them humming in the transformers
high on the poles I didn't understand I thought it might be God
you weren't there you didn't hear but just because you can't
say I didn't do you believe you're a scientist but afraid
to say no just say no we're the only ones in the room you wonder

why they speak through me water can only flow from the pacific
to the arctic ocean through the bering strait did you ever think
about that they want me to leave you can't make me stay here
they'll let me out they have ways better to let me go and someone
doesn't get hurt they can turn me into vapour into dust listen
listen if you'd only listen

My Early Love Life

I remember coming home
knowing I was in trouble
the minute I walked in the door.
Mr. and Mrs. Sanderson were there
sitting with my mother and the old man.
They had their daughters there, too,
Rose and Elizabeth,
so I knew for sure I was in deep shit.

The old man didn't waste any time.
He turned to Mrs. Sanderson.
Tell him what she told you!
Mrs. Sanderson's eyes shifted
over to the girls. They just stood there
with those fabled tits sticking out
and their eyes on the floor.

Mrs. Sanderson looked worse than I felt.
Her face was white and sickly.
She took a long time to speak.
Elizabeth, tell what you told me
about what this boy did to you.
The girl didn't look up.
You could hardly hear her. She said

He took me down by the creek
and he put his thing in me at first
it hurt and then it felt good
and then he peed in me
Jesus Christ, I *had* to fuck the stupid one!
Well, she was the one let me.

The old man hit me hard across the face then
before I had a chance to lie
and I could taste the blood and hear my mother
screaming but I jumped right up

beat it out the door
before the old man and Sanderson both could get at me.

Sanderson had that big knobby cane and the old man
wouldn't have stopped him using it.
It was already dark, they didn't have a chance
of catching me. I spent the night in a ditch
just outside town slipped back home
the next morning when they were gone to church
for my clothes and some money.
I knew where they kept their stash.

They weren't the forgiving kind.
I never went back, never saw them again.
I was pretty young then but I've done okay
in all the years since.
All I really regret is Rose.
I could have fucked her too.

Walking the Dog

I'm walking my dog
as I usually do this time of evening,

carrying his leash, letting him run free.
The dog is obedient, comes when I call,

no harm in giving him a bit of freedom.
A van pulls up beside me,

two people in the front seat,
a man, the driver, and a woman,

his wife, I presume. The driver leans over
and gestures with his fingers

to me to come closer. He's delusional,
thinks he's the King of England,

summoning one of his vassals.
You're letting your dog run free, he tells me.

I walk over to the passenger side
and look at them through the open window.

Did you hear what I said? Your dog is loose.
The dog is a half-block ahead, sniffing at something.

I stare at them until they start to get nervous,
then step in front of the van and take out my notebook.

There's no plate on the front but I write down
the make and colour, then walk to the back

and record the license number. I could kill them both
right now, there's no one around

but I want to make them sweat a little.
They must live around here. I'll find them,

let some time pass before they start getting
fleeting glimpses of a dark figure across the street,

phone calls in the night, someone breathing
on the other end, bags of dog shit

in the front yard. People make me sick.
Why wouldn't they just mind their own business?

The woman didn't say anything
but she saw me, knows my face. That's

bad luck on her part. Anyway, she deserves it,
marrying an asshole like that.

Evenings

After Angela left
I'd sit in restaurants for hours

newspaper open, listening to conversations
in the next booth or from down the counter.

I'd go to bars, sports events, any place
people would gather,

I filled blank spaces with the lives of others.
It was easy. I was nondescript.

No one noticed me. My hearing improved.
I was careful and used discretion.

There was this middle-aged couple who'd meet
Tuesday and Thursday afternoons;

they'd arrive at the restaurant separately,
almost to the minute, he first.

They sat, whenever possible, in the same booth.
We're all creatures of habit. If the adjacent booth

was unoccupied I'd slip into it,
crunch down with my coffee and crossword.

I learned all their intimate secrets,
the extent of her treachery, the pleasure she took

in her deceit, whispering, laughing
at the humiliation of her blameless husband.

I followed them to their respective homes,
her first, him the following Thursday.

I knew everything; where they worked,
the names of their spouses, the numbers of their children.

Her name was Christine, his was John but he went by Jack.
They were my first.

I started keeping odd hours, going out late at night.
It was September and darkness came early.

I'd go to the park and walk around, searching for a suitable spot
in the foliage, close to a bench or wall.

I'd settle in, well before dark, and wait.
It was mostly teenagers, smoking and gossiping

with the boys endlessly trying to cop a feel.
What they had to say was boring and uninteresting

but I was trapped in my self-made prison.
Sometimes, I'd hit pay dirt. This is a small town

and prominent citizens are easily recognizable,
even in the dark. One night,

a well-known businessman and his giggling
secretary or office girl or whoever she was

stumbled to the bench that nestled
next to my hiding place. There was a moon

and I could see everything. They had been intimate
for some time because he had his hand up her skirt

the moment they sat down. He was married
and from their conversation it was evident

that she was, too. It was all rather sordid, the two of them
on the ground and she calling out his name

in her ecstasy. I have the sounds of their rutting on tape
but it upsets me and I seldom listen to it anymore.

Lying together in a dark, peaceful corner of the leafy
public park, they could never have imagined me.

A couple of weeks later, I bought a night vision monocular,
digital, so I could see in black and white. I could have

bought one of the cheaper, analog types
but the green resolution was too creepy.

It was a bit creepy as it was, seeing people and listening to them
as if they were sitting in my living room.

This technological aid was not without its dangers. The lens,
as well as my eye would be damaged by any light source

and I lived in fear of a flashlight. I took the precaution
of joining the local chapter of the natural history society.

That way, I could explain away the monocular
and the tape recorder. I would be there

observing night birds and recording their cries.
Although the pain and emptiness of Angela's departure

has abated, I can't seem to stop.
I've amassed a hoard of valuable information.

It's all recorded, one way or another
and its secret nature makes it all the more powerful.

I have to say an unfortunate incident
the other night has changed everything.

At the same time, things are now much more exciting.
Until now, the prospect of being discovered

has not caused me much concern. I reasoned
that most guilty couples would flee in terror

if they spotted me, especially if I were wearing my balaclava.
Well, on this particular night, what I imagine

was an erring husband saw me through the bushes
just as the moon moved from behind a cloud.

It must have been his first time because
instead of taking his girl by the hand and running off

he panicked and charged through the brush toward me.
I barely got away with my life. Now,

I carry this. I'm not young
and never was very robust.

Anyway, self-defense is not a crime.
I still say this is all down to Angela.

I should be home evenings, watching television
or reading or walking the dog. She took the dog.

Frogmen

I was at an outdoor pool
nice summer day.

A couple of kids, young guys,
maybe seven or eight years of age

were hanging around and I started bullshitting them
telling them how I used to be a frogman.

I think the name caught them
and I had to explain what that was.

I showed them how to dive down
and stick plastic explosives

to the hulls of enemy ships
blow them to fucking kingdom come.

The kids loved the idea
we were in the shallow end

and they started diving down, too.
Hell, we were frogmen together.

Then some fat broad comes over, starts yapping
about me teaching the kids to be violent,

said I was *aggrandizing war*
for Christ's sake

said she was going to report me
for using foul language in a public place.

I said, *Who are you, their mother?*
she says, *No, but you should leave those boys alone*

let them play by themselves and stop
filling their heads with such nonsense.

I said then in a real quiet voice, so the kids wouldn't hear,
so it wouldn't carry over the water

Lady, how stupid are you?
I'm giving these kids something their fathers should be doing.

I'm teaching them to be men, so they won't spend their lives
getting pulled around by the ears by some uptight bitch like you.

She huffed and puffed
said she was going to phone her husband.

Call him, I said, *I'll be waiting*
out there in the parking lot, but just remember

you were the one told him to come,
you'll be responsible for what happens to him.

You could see by her face that made her think.
I got dressed and hung around in the parking lot.

I doubted her husband would show and anyway
he was probably in the same physical shape as her.

Just in case, I picked up a couple of good-sized stones,
put them in my swim bag.

I'd ring his fucking chimes
while he was making his speech

while those kids were still diving down
lost in the real world.

Next Five

Old Bill claimed he got the paddle in Kingston,
says he got it for fighting but he went down
for armed robbery and they used to give it
for that kind of offence back then, gave it
for damned near everything. *Got ten,* he said,
five to start and five later, after you'd healed.
Worse than the fucking lash by a long shot.

I bought him a beer and he told me
it wasn't a paddle made of wood or anything
just a leather strap like the shaving strap
his old man used to use on him
when he wasn't sharpening his blade
only bigger and wider with holes punched in it.
Said his old man's strap never came close.

They'd blindfold you, tie you down to the bench.
It had leather pads on top and some big stupid guard
some moron bastard with his eyes
close together, would swing that paddle. Holy Jumping Jesus!
You always knew when it was coming
by the whistling noise and the cheeks of your ass
would tighten up but that didn't help a goddamned bit.

By the time they were done that five you were
truly bloody sorry for whatever it was you did
but a couple of days later
you were wishing you'd taken the whole ten
'cause you'd be thinking every fucking waking hour
about the next five.

The Mark of Cain

It's there in the morning,
a red mark the size of a dime
about two inches above my left eye.
It must be a sign,
something internal,
a blood vessel ruptured,
maybe an impending stroke –
penalty for those power laps in the pool.
Or an omen, notice of the day of reckoning
due me for my misbegotten youth.
It looks angry in the mirror, maybe it was
a drop of holy water did it.

The mark stays livid all day. I take it shopping.
People look at me in the mall.
I've become interesting; it's given me character,
like a dueling scar, my own rugged beauty spot.
I start to think it's nothing to worry about,
maybe even a good thing, the darkness
before a glorious dawn, like the time
Freddy Davidson fell and broke his leg
chasing me because I'd let the air
out of his tires or those
girls who thankfully
weren't pregnant after all.

It could be a great conversation piece
leading to stories about how I was grazed
with the bullet from a zip gun
saving a beautiful woman in the Toronto subway
or how my memory was burned away
by the long, crooked finger of a Zulu witch doctor
and now I can't remember how I ended up here
in the wilderness.

Adventures in Literature

When I was sixteen or seventeen
I read a story about a young man
corrupted by an older woman
who took him into the bedroom
she shared with her husband
shedding her clothes, laughing *What's the matter,*
haven't you ever seen a naked woman?

and he told her about finding the body
of a neighbour lady, a friend of his mother's
nude on her bed, strangled
with her own stocking.
There was no more laughter.
She pulled him down, into her bed
and as they made love her eyes
turned upward in their sockets
and she cried out *Kill me! Kill me!*

Afterward, she said to him
It wasn't you, was it?
and I sought out women
old enough and worn enough
and told them the story
as if it were my own, igniting
a spark of fear and danger
that made the blood rush wild

and cold in their veins.
None ever shouted, *Kill me!*
but one placed my hands
around her neck
and held them there
the whole time.

My Brother, Who I Looked Out for When We Were Kids

it was the tenth or the fiftieth
or the hundredth time
we brought him to the house
and cleaned him and fed him
and called his sponsor who didn't even want
to bother with him any more he said
he just wants to kill himself, there's nothing
you can do

and it was true, he looked like death, his skin
translucent, waxy   I said
you've got to get straight, get a job
and he laid there on the couch and said
I can't work out in the cold
I need an office job, an executive job
and that was bad, because I knew then
how hopeless things were

and he promised, for the hundredth time
to stop drinking and to go to the meetings
and we piled groceries into bags
and I drove him to the place where he lived
Wong said he owed last month's rent
and I paid that and the next month in advance
and I made him give me a receipt

he sold the groceries
because somebody saw him an hour later on the street
with his woman and said
by the way they were falling down
they must have got hold of something
it was a thing to crush you
we couldn't do anything and we couldn't stop trying

finally, my father came down from the Coast
he ended up drinking with him, told us

we didn't do anything to help him
when he said that he was lucky he was my father
he bought two tickets, took him back
to Vancouver on the train
afterward he wrote a letter, saying things
hadn't worked out saying he'd been
wrong, saying he'd left and he didn't
know where he was

a long time later he wrote again telling us
about how he'd come across
a newspaper item, just a few lines
buried in a back page that said he died
alone in some flophouse and that the city
had buried him as having
no known next of kin

I wrote my father a letter, he needed something
was looking for something
from me and told him we all had tried
I said he had taken that wrong turn
and but for the grace of God
it could have been me
it was nobody's fault

The Visitor

It's pouring rain, getting late, and I'm sitting here
in the kitchen, thinking about staggering off to bed
when this truck pulls into my drive-way, headlights shining
through the window of my living room.

I know the guy can see me at the kitchen table
and for what seems like a long time
nothing happens. The guy doesn't move or shut off the motor
or turn off his headlights and I can't even tell

if it's one guy or two in the cab and Jesus Christ Almighty
stuff starts going through my head and I'm trying to remember
if I screwed anybody's wife lately or messed with some asshole
in the bar and it occurs to me if he's got a rifle in there

I'm a perfect target
even with the lights down low
so I put down my coffee cup and move out of his view.
I think about ducking out the back and circling around

but he would have posted his buddy out there, anticipating
that kind of dumb panic move and I don't want a tire iron
behind the ear. When I sneak a peek through the bathroom window
he's turned his headlights out. It's like one of those horror movies

the kids watch only it's not too goddamned entertaining right now.
I could call the cops but what am I gonna say, *some guy's parked*
in my driveway? Anyway, I've got this baseball bat. If that fucker
comes through the door

Ten minutes, maybe fifteen gone by and still nothing.
I'm trying like hell to figure this out. Maybe
he's got the wrong house, maybe he thinks his old lady is in here.
No use swinging the door open and telling him she's not here

that's the same thing I'd say if she was. A fucking dilemma

no two ways about it. Not a sound from out there. Nothing
behind that windshield. I don't mind a guy coming at me
with his fists or a broken bottle but this, this is bullshit.

He doesn't like me much. I don't know why.
Maybe I said something or wrote something he didn't like.
Maybe I looked at him sideways or looked at his girlfriend
or maybe it's just chemistry. Some people don't like each other.

It's just the way things are. You don't have to like everybody, otherwise
how could we have wars or sports teams for Christ's sake?
It's the face he brings, even when he's smiling and you start giving back
every chance you get, laughing loudly at inappropriate moments

standing stone-faced, looking past him when you have to say hello
the brush-fingers handshake and you wait for your chance
to take the fucker down although he's never done anything
except not like you. Well, too goddamned bad.

Then, I think I hear something at the front door. Maybe
he's trying the lock. The door has one of those peep-holes
and I'm just about to look through it when I remember a story
I read, about a hit-man who knocked on a mark's door

then stepped to one side, knowing the guy would look
and the killer put his gun
up to the peep-hole, shot the guy right in the eye.
There's no way I can look and I back into the shadows.

Nearly an hour now, so I know this is no joke, not just
somebody horsing around and I say it out loud
well two can play that game, asshole. I know the house
and you don't. I still have the baseball bat

and I'll be damned if I don't start to get a hard on

thinking about how it would feel
coming down on his skull, all the tension
exploding into a thousand fucking pieces

and then I start thinking about what to do with him
and his goddamned monster truck
but those are details. There's a long night ahead.
It's pitch dark and raining and the adventure's

got hold of me. I unlatch the door and it swings open.
I smell the rain and feel the cool breeze
and tremble a little from the blood rushing through me.
It's his move. *He's the one started it.*

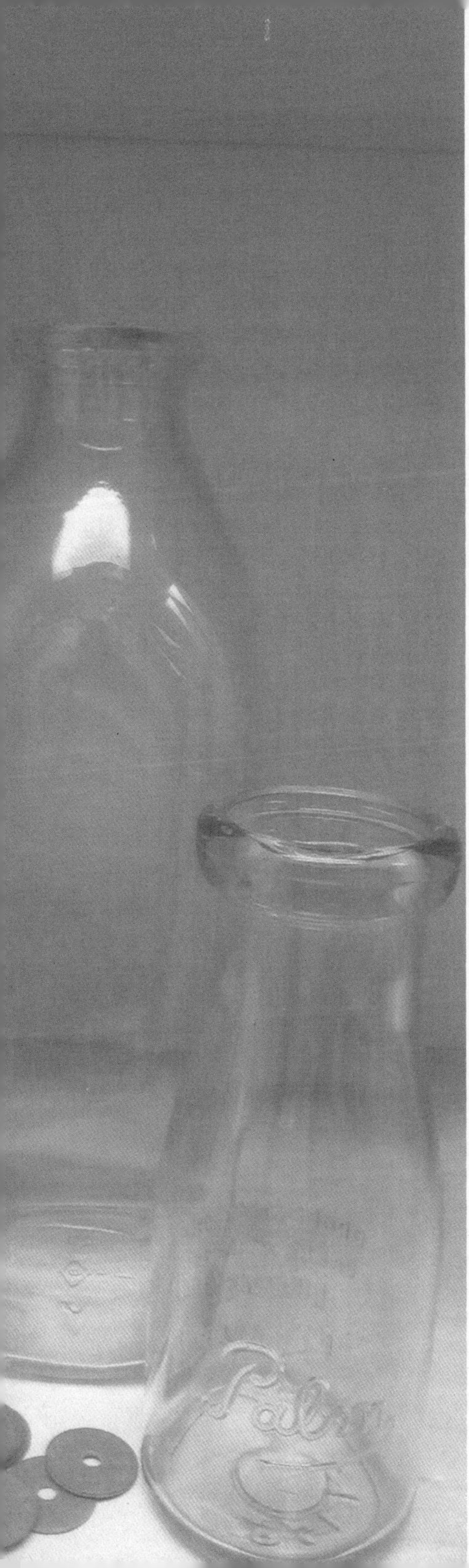

Memories

The Cliffs

surprised they still loom so high
after all these years not like

the bedrooms and shrunken yards
of this neighbourhood

remembering how we'd rappel
to the CN tracks below

trusting the skinny arms
and the heels dug in anchoring

that frayed piece of rope somebody found
then climbing up again and down

rescuing blown spies from the Nazis
until the anchors protested.

I follow the twisted path
up the cut to the thicket

where we'd sit and smoke
hidden from all the world

and climb to the prairie above
that dry ocean still rustling in the wind

the Healey place
the last jutting headland

guarding that vast expanse
under that vast expanse

Close Cover Before Striking

Every pack of cigarettes used to come with a free
book of matches, so when I pushed thirty-five
cents over the glass counter-top in McDaniels'
News Stand Bennie Schwartz gave me a pack of Camels
and that book of matches.

I'd picked Camels because the ads said they were "toasted"
and that sounded good, like breakfast. I'd never smoked
a cigarette but I'd seen how guys would break the seal
on the pack with a thumbnail and shake one out. I took the pack
outside and broke the seal and shook out a cigarette
and put it between my lips. I cocked my head to one side
and looked tough.

It was early evening and already dark.
Still, the alley would be better. No one would see me there.
This was a private moment. The blackness
of the alley enveloped me and I opened my book
of matches and struck one, anticipating the sweet
aroma of toasted tobacco. I was about to enter
the world of the sophisticated.

The night exploded into searing light and fumes of phosphorus
that burned in my head and nose and eyes as I stood, staring
at the ball of fire in my hand, trying to understand
what was happening. Finally, I dropped what was left
of my book of matches, but it was much too late.
The flame had burned my thumb

beyond recognition, as they say in the movies.
By the time I got to the streetlight
a shiny black-brown crust was already forming,
sealing the pain inside, the phosphorus burning
down to the bone. I'd never thought before
about having a bone in my thumb.

The pain was excruciating. For the first time,
I knew what that word really meant. Christ, what an idiot!
On the way home snow started to fall
and I gratefully held out
my thumb to catch the flakes.

I'd like to say that blackened thumb
cured me, but I soon graduated to a pack a day.
I became a Virginia man.
Got myself a Zippo lighter.
I loved the way it would stay lit
the flame horizontal
in the strong Saskatchewan wind.

Fences

It's warmed up and the sun is shining
and I get this nice Saturday feeling

I had as a kid, wheeling my bike
down to the Y, a tin of sardines in my jacket

for lunch all those guys running around
jumping on tables, I think it was some initiative

to give kids something to do weekends
something to do, that was a laugh,

that was why we'd get out of the house early
before the wood chopping, coal hauling

weeding the garden, there was no lawn to speak of
thank Heaven. There were always old fences,

this one between Koziol's garage
and the neighbour's, where we'd sit wedged, knees up,

uncomfortable but away, just outside the periphery
of parents and busybodies. Old garages, the paint

faded to almost nothing, enclosed by weeds seeded so often
year after year they had squatters' rights.

This alley, narrow and dusty, from where
we lured the Weston sisters out of their back yard

and took them down by the creek. Nothing bad happened,
they liked it too, the adventure of sitting in the cave

we'd hollowed from the bank, giggling as they watched us
roll and smoke the gone-to seed dock we called Indian tobacco.

We sat in the culvert that carried the slow lazy creek under the road
all night after Gordy McWilliams fired a .22 into the water

and a kid on the far bank tumbled down the hill,
a bullet in the cheek of his ass. No one in this neighbourhood

ever had a fence that could keep anything in or out; they were
required, like front porches or those narrow black mailboxes

with the wire part at the bottom for the newspaper. Everything
that occurred or was to occur in my life is here

in this neighbourhood, with its falling fences and its schools
and creeks and sled-riding hills. This place

makes me think of Faulkner, its meaning
always just beyond.

River Park

The river flowing silently, long shadows
of trees from the far side arriving over water

to the bank below where I sit
taking the sun

imagined whirr
of a dragonfly's wings

hovering like a blue daydream
at the river's edge.

Not easy to guess
the age of these trees

gnarled and contorted by time
and the wind

but they were here when I was young
and will be here when I am gone and when

my sons are gone. Time is the least thing
to consider here, some of the benches with plaques

the names of men and women who came
for the silence and to watch the river flow.

So much bound up in those silences
and in the slow passing of the river.

The sun goes down. The trees settle in the darkness.
The river moves on, reflecting the silver light of the moon.

Soft summer days when branches were green and supple
days when we were young

and came to River Park
and laughed at old men sitting on benches.

Stopped at the Traffic Light across from William Grayson School

And who knows, or guess, what, long ago, happened there?
Robert Penn Warren – *Lessons in History*

that Grade Eight classroom
me, the new kid, starting cold

after Easter break the teacher,
intense, with a brush cut

asking us to name the Cabinet
of the British Government, took *Prime Minister*

and when the process stalled, I stood
and said *Chancellor of the Exchequer*

His face soured and he dismissed me
with a flick of his wrist *We're not*

talking he said of *minor positions.*
I'm looking for the important offices

and I opened my mouth to say something
and closed it again and sat down

and the kids blinked and looked around
waiting for the recess bell

and I blinked and looked around
and went outside with them and can't remember

if there was a soft spring breeze
or snow on the ground

Johnny Weissmuller's Moose Jaw

Every morning I walk across Africa.
Not all of it. A country, maybe,

or part of a country, some are quite large.
This lazy muddy green-banked river

could be the set for all those Tarzan movies
I lived in Saturday afternoons at the Royal.

I use the map that was pinned to the wall
in my first-grade classroom,

a quarter of the world in red
and a picture of a Neilson chocolate bar

in the lower right-hand corner.
The map is long out of date

and the world has changed. Countries
have merged or split, have new names,

but I still like Gold Coast,
Ivory Coast, Basutoland

and places that were no longer around by the time
my map was printed, The Oil Rivers, New Republic,

Transvaal and German East Africa.
It's good, though, that some things never change;

Africa's rivers still flow deep and dark and muddy,
are still named the Congo, Niger, Zambezi,

the Limpopo, the Blue Nile and the White,
but I never travel by boat. I walk.

I carry a supply of water
and keep my eyes open for a pool of shade.

I've learned to be cautious along the streams
and river banks. The crocodile can lie motionless

beneath a few inches of water. You won't see it
but it can see you and if you come just one millimeter

too close, you're gone. *Disappeared in Darkest Africa.*
Sounds romantic but it really isn't.

I hope to come upon Stanley or Livingstone one morning
just at that dip through the caraganas. No luck yet,

but one day a war-party of Zulus
crossed the veldt on one of their 50-mile runs

in the scorching heat. Where else
are you going to see something like that?

All along my walk dogs bark from back yards,
giving away their positions. I'm amazed the jackals

or hyenas haven't gotten them by now. The handle
from an old spade provides me with a walking stick and

serves as protection against snakes. Heat waves
rising from the river blur my vision.

I retreat into the shade,
wipe the sweat band of my

pith helmet, check the safety
on this beautifully-balanced rifle,

clouds of insects buzzing
in the suffocating heat of River Park,

when the *splash* of something falling into the water
a small helpless child or pretty girl

alerts the reptilian thing in the weeds
and *O my God, my gun's jammed!*

when I hear his cry
from high in the canopy overhead

Ahhh Eeeahhh Eeahhh Eeahhh Eeahhh
and suddenly, thrillingly

he swings in that famous arc over the river
knife clenched fiercely in his teeth

hair falling into those strange slanted Teutonic eyes
and drops to the monster's back. I stand, enthralled

never doubting the outcome
as they roll over and over together, the knife

flashing in the sunlight as it plunges, again and again
into the soft white belly of the beast.

God, how I loved him!
all the movie Tarzans after him

wore those little pull-on *slippers*
for Christ's sake!

My Father's Hat

I bought a hat, a fedora
and bent down the brim

on the front right side and trained it
with a binder clip

The first time my sister saw it she said
My God, you look just like Dad

and I looked in the mirror
and she was right

and I thought about all those
little pieces of paper he used to fill

with strange cryptic columns
of numbers and I thought about

how one day he threw everything away
his job, years of service

sold the house, moved us far away
from our school and our friends

like we were being punished for something
like he was punishing himself

It was hard at first
but we were young and resilient

and bounced back, some of us
and I learned not to blame him

or myself or the world and searched
until I found all the little pieces

and put them back together and never
threw away anything important

and I remembered, years later
stopping to visit him in Vancouver

sitting mostly silent until a decent interval
had passed, getting up, saying

I wanted to walk along English Bay
while I was here and he, surprising me

offered *I'll go with you*
and as we watched the tide he said

You've done all right for yourself
which is about as close as he ever came.

That's Me in the Picture

Page 189 of *The Moose Jaw Book;*
the interior of the Public Library, 1964,
Ida Cook and Mary Jefferson
and me, that unidentified patron
leaning on the desk
beneath the elegant marble rotunda.

I was slim, with all that dark hair
and those black framed glasses
everyone wore back then.
I'd forgotten what I looked like
until I saw that photograph.

I don't remember anyone taking that photo
or maybe I pretended not to notice
but there I am, where I used to go
locked for a moment in that important place.

I look relaxed, confident
with my elbow on the desk, upstairs
after all those years; the children's section
in the basement the only part of the library
where kids were allowed. Down there, too,
the lavatories, doors
with opaque windows of wire mesh
sandwiched between glass
and dank toilets, the plumbing
looking exactly the way you'd think
plumbing would look
if for some reason you were to think about plumbing.

The worst was, kids
could take out only one book per visit
and I can't remember a time
I made it all the way home
without finishing my book

even in winter when I had to sit
on a cold bench in Crescent Park.

I sometimes doubled back
hoping to check out another book
before closing time.
The librarian would look over her glasses
examine the returned book closely, certain
I'd dropped it in a puddle.

I remember my day of arrival
when I got an adult card and could walk gingerly
on the glass floor upstairs. I learned the card index
and the Dewey Decimal System in a world
all the sweeter for those years of denial.
I still take out armfuls, never getting enough.

Ida Cook, who's also in the photo
ran that library gently and efficiently for years
as *Interim Head Librarian.*
They were never to give her the title;
she didn't have *Bachelor of Library Science*
after her name.

That's me in the picture.
You can say it's not or say it's you
but I know better.

The Leopard

The government elevators morph
into Victoria Falls through the smoke
from forest fires in the north, mist

rising from the Zambezi River below, summoning
The Falls' African name, *Mosi-oa-Tunya,*
the smoke that thunders.

Lines of ants swarm across the pavement at my feet
like a herd of wildebeest
photographed from above in a Cessna,

while to the North, across the rail yards, termite towers
dominate the skyline at Cypress Paving
looking for all the world like hills of sand and gravel.

I pass a beautiful black girl, ingenuously naked
but for a loincloth and a necklace of bones,
a bundle perfectly balanced on her head.

The sun is high and my water almost gone. Sweat
runs down my face and neck. The rutted, stony road
is a barren river bed in this dry season.

I should be home, eating lunch
in my air-conditioned kitchen but each day
I stall a little longer,

waiting for dusk to fall, waiting
for the sound of drums from beyond the mountains
and the cough of the leopard in the dark.

Women

Hornet

occasional red brake lights
pinpointing the squat sturdy Hornet

parked in moonlight
Saturday night,

dusty smell of the upholstery
soft night air   some girl's laughter,

radio playing warm
vacuum-tube music

through tiny speakers   green light
glowing from the dashboard,

cigarette smoke
drifting from the driver's window,

wind soughing in the dry grass   dawn
just below the horizon.

Anatomy of a Glance

Dinner theatre, holiday time
all the tables filled.

She with her family, I'm guessing,
father, mother, sisters

and through the noise, swirling waiters
people passing to and fro

the still moment of her face a photograph
the shutter opening and closing.

She gazes with a woman's mild contained interest
maybe I've spilled something on my shirt.

I make her out to be a university student
home for the Christmas season

intelligent, aloof not cold
just matured   a bit removed from the rest of the family

and I remember, in black and white,
a Naked City episode on TV

from perhaps 40 years ago
a young woman, much like her,

an old man, much like me,
the actor Luther Adler in a starched white shirt

his sad, homely face, hopeless
their plight, hopeless the point of the sub-plot.

The waiter brings coffee
and my wife asks for decaf.

I relax, taste the wine in my glass, satisfied
with the barriers the world constructs.

The writer in me settles down
to wander through the performance.

and as the show is about to begin
the mother turns suddenly

scans the tables, sensing
something

Photograph of Myrna at 18

She sits, slim and beautiful
her arm in mine

smiling at the camera with that look
Annette Bening spent a lifetime

trying to achieve. I'm wearing
a white dinner jacket

my first and last, rented of course
and she, well, she's spectacular.

Looking now at this photograph
it occurs to me I was right

to be relentless
to have had the instincts

of a Bengal tiger
stalking, prowling

holding her face in my claws
hypnotizing her with yellow eyes.

One month, one week, one day
and she might have found

someone else. I know she wanted
to have a career, wanted to travel

but young men can't wait
and know

it's all in the moment
like this photograph.

Smoke

I used to smoke. Cigarettes, a pipe for awhile,
the odd cigar, but mostly cigarettes.

I smoked in the house, in the car with the kids
in the back seat, smoked in restaurants, at gatherings,

on the bus, in the street, everywhere. I'd light up
before breakfast, after lunch, after supper, after sex,

smoke over a coffee or a drink, smoke
at dances, in bars, in stores, at PTA meetings.

I smoked while reading and shaving and
on the can. I smoked at work, everybody

smoked at work. I could roll my own with one hand
scratch the match with my thumbnail, flip the butt

in a perfect arc. I smoked in poolrooms and in hospitals
and at the drive-in theatre. I even smoked in a downtown

movie theatre a couple of times but that was a bit much,
even for me. When I did my budget at the end of the month

and when I used to paint on canvas, I'd light a cigarette,
set it down in the ash tray and forget about it

then light another. I smoked in the heat and the cold
and the rain. I would have smoked in the swimming pool

if that were possible. I smoked in doctors' waiting rooms,
watched movies where people smoked in court rooms

and in dark alleys with their collars turned up.
If you wanted to look tough you stuck a cigarette in the corner

of your mouth and squinted one eye when the smoke drifted
into it and when you walked a girl to her door after a first date

and didn't know what to say you could always
light a cigarette.

Frankenstein

remembering the headlights
bouncing up one of those paths

branches clawing at the windows
the girl close

her skinny legs, her hair
shining in the light of the dashboard

parking at the very edge
of the river, motor idling, the radio

indistinct, how they talked
about the movie, half-expecting

The Monster to come lurching
out of the trees into the silver night

hearing himself say, as if it mattered,
that in the book it was called *The Creature*

never T*he Monster,* that term coming from the movie
and wasn't it odd that in the movie

they changed Dr. Frankenstein's Christian name
from Victor to Henry? And how she smiled

and stretched and turned toward him
taking off her top the way

girls never did back then, upsetting
his careful plan

as something moved
past the window of the car

past the corner of his eye
in the darkness

369 High Street East

I find the address where she lived all those years ago
in an old Henderson Directory and at first I'm puzzled
because there's nothing in this block
between Third Avenue and the CN track

until I realize the house has been razed,
grass and the relentless weeds covering every trace
of those small breasts in the darkness
the long brown hair and her mouth,

laughing as we traded that wad of gum
back and forth, an intimacy
between us. I can't imagine
meeting her now or how we'd look

at one another or what we'd have to say
if I happened to be standing beside this vacant lot
as she drove slowly by
in sunglasses and with her window rolled down…

167 Hochelaga East

The house is still there on that quiet genteel street
the same glassed-in porch, new windows
different siding, that wide white boring stuff
not the shiplap I remember or was it green stained
cedar shingles? An air conditioner now
at the side of the house, something unheard of
back then. I'd stop in the summer heat
throw my bike down on the hard
knobby lawn and she'd come out
to talk to me or sometimes
the house would watch silently
until I went away. I never knocked.

Her name was Mona Eaton and her hair
was red, dark red, almost brown. I don't know
how I met her, she didn't go to my school.
I delivered papers in her neighbourhood
maybe she spoke to me one day I never
would have said the first word. After that,
I'd stop whenever I was going by and even rode down
to her house on purpose. Her father
was a furrier. He had a store on Main Street.
He came into the glassed-in porch one day
when Mona was sitting on her front step
and I was sitting on her lawn.

Her father wore glasses and had a moustache.
His face was angry. He didn't say anything.
No one said anything and when he went inside
Mona Eaton told me I'd better go and she got up
from the step and went into her house
through the glassed-in porch. I never saw her again.
I remembered the street and the glassed-in porch
and the lawn. Henderson's Directory lists her
as a lab student at the Providence Hospital in 1960.
I go by her house from time to time.

1957

What would have happened
if I'd have just gone back
the next day and quietly asked Joanie out
maybe for a Coke, she'd have liked that,
and talked to her and told her
she didn't have to do this?

I've thought about that
over the years, wondered
what I would have done
if she'd have stared at me like I was an idiot,
some deranged white knight riding
to save her when all she wanted to do
was give the only thing she had to offer

like she did that day, early fall
with the first wet snowflakes of the year
hissing on the hood of the Ford
as we pulled up in front of her house.

Grover said he could get us fixed up
and had driven to her house
and her mother had welcomed us
and invited us in and had called up the stairs
for Joanie to come down

and she came down, pulling on a sweater
neither sullen nor excited
nor happy nor sad
and got into the front seat of the Ford
sitting between us.

She was thin and quiet and shy,
with pasty skin and poor, thin clothes.
She looked as if she felt she deserved this
and didn't speak and rode between us

into the park, the afternoon sky dark,
threatening more snow.

Grover parked and told me to go for a walk
and I walked along the river, the leaves
wet and yellow under my feet.
When he blew the horn I went back.
They were in the front seat

and Grover asked me if I wanted to get fixed up.
She said it would be okay he said
She looked over at me and nodded
and I looked at the ground
and said, *No, not today,* and climbed into the car
not knowing what else to do.

We took her home and let her off
and she went into her house and we drove away.
The whole thing couldn't have taken
more than a half-hour. I told Grover
I had some things to do and he shrugged
and let me off near my place.

I didn't like to see a girl, any girl,
treated like that but it wasn't up to me
to watch out for her, I would have been
told to butt out, to mind my own business.
There were lots of guys besides Grover
hanging around there.

I wasn't looking to get my eyes
blackened for sticking my nose in,
for spoiling a good set-up.
I would have been accused
of wanting her for myself –
the first thing to cross their minds.

I never saw her again but I heard some
of what happened to her and it was about
what you'd expect would happen to a girl like that.
I guess she ended up where she was born to end up.
I don't think about her anymore.

At the Fair

We didn't mention the woman
to our mothers. They had forbidden us

to go anywhere near the Fair
with all the warnings

about avoiding crowds
in the time of the polio scare

She was outside in the sunshine
with throngs of people passing by

and as we stood there, mesmerized,
she smiled and talked to us.

We were amazed that she could speak.
Her eyes were blue.

She told us she had children of her own,
a boy and a girl

a few years older than we were.
I remember their names,

Ross and Mary Rose. She said
they were far away, at school,

that she didn't see them often
and started to cry. The iron lung

looked like a big water heater and she
seemed like a robot with just her face

talking. I thought about how people
talk with their eyes as well as their mouths

but also with their hands and arms
and shoulders and she must have caught

what I was thinking because she said
she wished she could hold our hands

and she cried some more. Two people
in white coats came, a doctor and nurse

they looked like, and the nurse reached in
a slot by the side of the iron lung

and did something and told us the lady
needed to rest now and we went away

but I'm glad we were there. That woman
just needed someone to talk to.

Women are Funny

I'd read these dirty books
and then try stuff, you know,

see what they liked.
Older women, the married ones,

liked everything, couldn't get enough;
the younger ones, single girls,

would get scared or disgusted.
I'd see them on the street

or in cafes, in groups, whispering.
God knows what they were telling each other.

Women are funny, they'll tell each other stuff
a man would fucking *never* tell another man

but, you know, eventually, if I tried hard enough
and jumped through all the hoops

I'd get another chance and I could tell
by those side-long glances

she'd thought things over and decided
that maybe she was now   intrigued.

Bike Talk

They like to say *No Worries* because
that's what the Aussies say.

It's like *Cool* or *Catch you later, Man*
but those aren't in vogue any more

and even if they were
they couldn't be used.

Bike talk, as needful as the wheels
that carry them fearlessly over

the ramps and up the walls
of the concrete canyons. and the helmet, well,

they get that, but their disdain
for knee and elbow pads

is just as needful.
Restricts them, they say. Maybe they believe it.

The price they pay is not to show
it hurts when they fall, when they *wipe*

and they learn not to notice the scrapes
the blood streaming.

Ori is six, has his own *Fit,* four pegs,
one back wheel brake.

He's already a prodigy in the bowl
going over the spine

practicing 180s, rail hops, working the nerve
for a nose wheelie

pretending not to hear, properly ignoring
the accolades of the big kids.

Every day he learns new moves
takes more chances, rides closer to the edge

every bit the young Maasai warrior
approaching his lion.

The Window

It would do no good to knock.
There is no door, only the window.

Inside, the people live as required, drinking from glasses,
walking backward on their hands at frequent intervals.

Quite remarkably, a young woman comes to stand beside the
window. Safely,
she sees her own reflection sent back by the night.

There is nothing out here in the darkness;
only the rain, beating soundlessly against the glass.

Girls

girls we'd entice into cars
stopping at the Swing-Inn or Ike's

girls in jeans or pedal-pushers
who acted tough and asked for cigarettes

but as the pale moon rose
in the late night sky would beg

to be taken home, mothers or landladies
always at the gates

girls with trusting eyes and perfect faces
we'd neck with before we even knew their names

and try the rest, not because there was a chance
but because it was expected

and eventually drive them home
to Elvis or Little Richard

on the car radio, with the empty feeling
that we'd probably never see them again

or, if we did, they'd be with some other guys
or with a group of girls,

laughing
behind their hands

The Dead

Only the dead have seen the end of war.
— Plato

For the nut-case with a revolver
you'll need some distance, a rifle,
preferably with a scope and tripod.
Remember to *breathe* and squeeze the trigger.

A well-thrown grenade can take out a sniper
if you have a reasonable approximation
of where he is. Bazookas and flame-throwers
are terrifyingly effective.

We could continue this forever; rocket-launchers,
tanks, artillery, jet planes, guided missiles,
atomic bombs, hydrogen bombs, but we just
keep getting farther and farther apart.

I prefer the brawl at the country dance,
both of us half-drunk, tasting blood,
feeling our noses, trying to determine
whether they've been broken, ruining
our good looks forever

and getting up, dusting off our clothes,
shaking hands and laughing
because the girl has dumped us both, gone
with the guy from Regina in the convertible.

Writing

Becoming Charles Bukowski

The widow next door
gave us an old tire, said
maybe we could chop it up
to burn in the stove.

You ever try to chop up a tire
at forty below? I was lucky
I didn't cut my goddamned
leg off with that axe.

That would have made it even harder
to bail all that sewage out of the basement,
one of the few times the old man
and I did something together.

As it was, I had to be the one
to figure out we were just
recycling shit back through
that broken sewer pipe

You could get ten loaves of bread
or three pounds of hamburger
back then for a dollar if
you had a dollar.

I walked the two-and-a-half miles to Mulvey School
every day, pretended to walk home for lunch
on days I had no lunch. Portage was close,
you could keep warm in the Bay or Eaton's until one o'clock.

A few guys had a different pair of strides
for every day and three-speed bikes
but most were like me. The girls wore school
uniforms, sexier than they knew or maybe they did know.

Kids made out they were tough, but I already knew
there was always somebody tougher
or faster or smarter so I got along
but kept mostly to myself

and read a lot of detective and crime magazines
and made up my mind to stay out of jail.
It's almost always just a matter
of using your head.

Some guys did go to jail,
a few more died in car accidents,
but most, unless their fathers owned businesses,
were destined for jobs on the railway

or in the foundries or stockyards
and I could've gone that way, too, I guess
but for some goddamned strange reason I don't know,
it was just something came into my head,

I lit out hitchhiking, jumping freights,
got my head knocked in a couple times
by those big meathead railroad dicks,
Christ, they were tough bastards!

Ended up here in San Francisco.
It wouldn't have been the same
driving down, even if I had a car
or buying a bus ticket, I mean,

it wouldn't have had the same *cachet*,
the same *smell*. Be grateful
for everything that happens.
I learned to navigate,

hung around coffee bars
slept on the streets.
Frisco was a helluva lot
warmer than Winnipeg.

I met some guys down by the docks.
Writers, they said they were. I told them
back where I come from,
this is the other side of the tracks.

They bought me drinks and something to eat,
said I was a true primitive.
I picked right up on that.
They took me to meetings,

parties, showed me to people
like I was something they'd found in the jungle.
I went along, the dumber they thought I was
the bigger advantage.

Hell, I even ended up marrying
a couple of those *patronnes of the arts,*
made them squeal, made them pay.
It sounded like something I'd do.

Rothko: Untitled (Black on Gray), 1969/70 New York, Guggenheim Museum

This dark painting
not depressing

done so soon before his
suicide

with its grays plunging
upwards   the line

sharply delineated (for
Rothko) into black

night, not menacing, just its natural
half of the world,

perhaps with cloud
cover masking the stars

over an ice rink
real ice, outdoors

with scratches and
striations from

skates or the
cold and with the light

coming up, somehow, from below
a whole city

of light   rising
to the whitening sky

Günter Grass Writes a Poem

I can't help but imagine you, Günter,
in your Waffen-SS uniform standing at the ready
while your runt of a leader ramped things up

loading more of those silent, compliant
freight cars with more and more bodies;
little children, babies, women, pregnant women

Jews, half-Jews, quarter-Jews, eighth Jews,
Poles, Gypsies, the feeble, the elderly
the sick, the halt, the lame, political prisoners

girls with long hair, anyone with a gold tooth
or a pair of socks to be stolen and kept adding categories
in lunatic urgency, knowing full-well

the war was lost and wanting, before the end,
to exterminate every single one
every drop of blood, every fucking chromosome.

On April 6, 1944, Klaus Barbie announced
a particularly successful operation in which a total
of 41 children, aged 3 to 13 had been caught.

A three-year old – *caught!* He listed their names and ages
before they were sent to Auschwitz. None survived,
no mention of them in your poem, Günter.

Louise Glück as Non-Fiction

In the Library I find her
sandwiched between
How to Train Your Dog
and *The Coming Global Superstorm:*
Louise Glück, Poems 1962–2012.

Maybe someone picked the book up
and set it down on the wrong shelf
thinking it was about astronomy
with that fuzzy mezzotint of Saturn
on the front cover and the back.

Perhaps a woman, fresh from her garden,
head brimming with peas carrots
and beef stock discovered, for a moment,
The Louise Glück Cookbook
big and substantial, sitting on the shelf.

It could have been mistaken
for biography: far-flung, larger than life, smoldering
with Hungarian-Jewish sensuality.
If you open it, you will find the Great Storm on Jupiter
or the smell of spices and freshly-baked bread
in your mother's kitchen or sisters
circling one another warily
like animals.

Room without Board

If you could say it in words there
would be no reason to paint.
Edward Hopper (1882–1967)

A small ad in the classified,
one short line
and a telephone number

a drawing, study
for a painting, the words
on a square of cardboard

in a fly-specked window, the figure
of a man in the foreground, his back
to the viewer, shoulders slumped

already imagining
the threadbare evenings, the electric
hot plate, probably illegal, the kind

with coiled wires always burning out,
the man an alcoholic, a drifter,
maybe just out of jail in a tattered suit

from the Sally Ann, broken,
no longer wanting to fight
no longer wanting to bother,

the years a jumble of images,
a carpenter or pipe fitter, maybe
someone in the business world

with a home, a loving wife and family
respect in the community, how it all
went wrong

but this is preliminary, the reason,
I suppose, why Rothko would sit for days
smoking cigarettes, staring at the wall

before rising suddenly,
attacking the canvas like a wild-eyed prophet,
creating miracles.

Sermons in Stones

And this our life exempt from public haunt,
Finds tongues in trees, books in the running brooks,
Sermons in stones, and good in every thing.
I would not change it.
Wm. Shakespeare: *As You Like It*

he performs a daily ritual
lifts the stones from their sand beds

in rectangular varnished boxes
cleans them with what he deems

the proper respect
carefully sets the stones aside

grooms the sand
with tiny wooden rakes

(each box having its own rake) replaces the stones
in different orientations

to placate the gods or bring good luck
he remembers reading somewhere

about the number of ways possible
to arrange eight books on a shelf

so that if you arranged the books
in a different pattern each day

it would take 40,320 days to arrange them in all possible orders
but that is as nothing

compared to the directions possible
for his stones to be placed

reflecting the vaguely Buddhist bent
of his daily renewal

the stones representing mountains
and the sand the sea

but he knew nothing of this
when he constructed his boxes

the stones speak to him
of different lives, far-away places

some having been gathered
in defiance of laws forbidding their removal

as if the laws of stones
had anything to do with men

he tells them things too
a way for him to remember

the Spartans drank their wine mixed with water,
twenty-to-one and were told by their women

to come home with their shields
or come home carried on them

the stones listen blindly he never sees their eyes
glaze over when he relates

the Bishop's confirmation of *The Iliad* in a Nutshell
he rakes the sand into orderly waves

sets the stones in positions he hopes
will be the sea-bird sounds of Sculthorpe's *Cello Dreaming*

while the sea glistens in the sun
and the stones rise like a choir.

~

Today I spent twenty minutes watching a butterfly
watching me back with its orange eyes

on long stalks as it sucked nutrients from the damp
soil in a seed pot, its proboscis moving from point

to point in a semi-circle with the grace
and agility of Fred Astaire's cane,

drawing goodness out of the soil along with
just enough moisture to make it happen

and I thought about the farmers in Manitoba
along the Emerson sub. burning stubble, the wind

fouling our ballast with topsoil, the land as flat
as a billiard table. Percy the Roadmaster said

the top-soil was 12 feet deep, so nobody worried
about a little being blown away and anyway

a world without soil would be a world without
wheat or much else and no need at all for a railway

and the winds would blow clean and fresh
over a vast quiet empty landscape of rock

but there is soil, with all those bodies
buried over the centuries slowly turning back

to carbon and nitrogen and calcium and phosphorus,
the stuff of good fertilizer, feeding the plants,

feeding the livestock, feeding us, so we can die
and be buried and continue the cycle and I remembered

dray horses pulling the honey-wagon down the alleys
and the grimy men who never smiled

trading empty pails for full ones through the flap
doors of the outhouses. They were called night soilers

but we only ever saw them in the daytime. Later on,
they were given a clanking old motor truck and they

just dumped the contents of the pails into a big tank.
One guy would stand on the deck and the other would

hand up pails. The pails had a handle on each side which
made it easier for the one on the ground to hoist it up but

the guy up top would grab the pail by one handle and
the pails were usually right full and heavy

so there was always some stuff slopping over.
It got on everything, the truck, the ground, the men.

One of the men had a red beard and lived in a house
beside the creek. He never washed. We could smell him

a block away. He'd go into the corner store on his way
home from work and buy bread and milk. He never spoke.

It was as if he was daring anyone to say something to him
and nobody ever did. I guess he didn't like his job much.

People looked down on the honey men but their work
was every bit as necessary as the butcher or the coal man

or the preacher as far as that goes. Nobody with an outdoor
toilet could do without them for very long. The farmer

who brought a load of manure for your garden was
a soiler as well, but he was coming in on the front end

and all the time I'm thinking about this, the butterfly
is staring, its wings slowly opening and closing and

it occurs to me this one could be a descendant of a butterfly
that fed on the soil of China during the Tang Dynasty,

it's not impossible, and I want to ask if Li Po is in there,
staring out at me with those pinpoint orange eyes

and I lean over, as close as I dare, and whisper
Is that you, Li Po?

What If This All Really Happened?

The ad for the auction contains the usual fare
sets of china, glassware, collectables, old furniture

fitness equipment never used and *so much more*
and I'm just about to toss it aside when I see

10K STAR OF DAVID RING and
NAZI CIGAR CASE.

The auction consists of the household of the late
Mrs. Marion Greenwood and for the rest of the week

my imagination won't leave me alone, ignited and stoked
through all those Saturday afternoon serials

in the shadows of the Royal Theatre. Was her husband
an S.S. Colonel living quietly all these years

unsuspected, under an assumed name? Did he take that ring
from the finger of some doomed soul in Mengele's line

offer the Herr Doktor a fat cigar from his swastika
adorned case, watch with amusement

as the smoke from their cigars drifted upward
to blend with the other?

What if some ragged starving Jew
scaled the ghetto wall one moonless night in Warsaw?

What if he snuck through the gate contorted
inside that old woman's famous bread cart

surviving against all odds, finding himself
at the end of the war attached to the Allied Army

at Nuremburg on orderly duty
guarding prisoners in their cells? What if

the cigar case once belonged to Hermann Goering
that corpulent John Vernon look-alike?

You'd be wise, Jew, he might have whispered through the bars
if they take you to America, to change your name.

There are photographs of the Reich-Marshall smoking Cuban cigars
as well as those decadent perfumed cigarettes. Imagine

the secret compartment where he kept his emergency
cyanide pill. Imagine

going to the auction and bidding
and buying that Nazi cigar case

and discovering the secret compartment
all these years later, a 10K Star of David ring, inside.

Music

Five Guitars

lounging on their stands, one
hanging on the wall

strings trembling humming
their bodies, those curves

women he remembers
backs svelte & shining

one voice bell-like
one sweet, caramel-mellow

another deep, twelve-stringed, resonant
calling her hypnotic siren drone

a fourth, dark and jazzy
trading octaves up and down in the smoky light

the last, sliding beneath his hands
anticipating him like a mistress

he tunes each in her turn
coaxing equal temperament

never demanding what they can give
when the moon is right they may deign to weep or sing

wail with voices harsh
the roughness of the blues *the blues*

he whispers, caresses them
seeking that conceptual moment

when acoustics and humidity are right
but they are temperamental

in the intervals
he waits

Improvisations

Improvisation, it turns out,
is as structured as the DNA molecule

locked to the melody by key or mode, a bond
broken only by a wrong note

and even that bent to the soloist's advantage
as he segues it into a short run

of the standard, vaguely recognized
by everyone in the audience, too fleeting

to be definitely pinned down
but worthy of an appreciative round of applause.

for all those bluesmen
on the sweltering Mississippi delta

jazz trumpeters blowing in the smoky clubs
of Chicago and Harlem the shadowy guitarists

anonymously
backing up the headliner on stage

the modes of C major
Ionian   *Dorian*

wine-dark and mysterious
take patience to understand

like algebra reward like algebra
patterned logical easily proven

(just try playing G Phrygian mode
over a D major melody)

or for dominant progressions
the minor pentatonic

with a flatted fifth so you can sliiiiiiide
over that blue note with a

sweet touch of tension
mmm mmmm!!

I think I've now played
every mode

in every key
over every song written

in the past fifty years
and you have to understand

starting so late in life
it's made me young again

with the secret pleasure
of knowing what most people

never stop to think about
The Boys of Summer

was scored in G but played
a half-tone lower

The Hours

Morton Feldman's *The Viola in My Life*
The music quiet and oh so slow

dark waters winding through River Park
atonal, disjointed, darkly hypnotic

floating, like I did when I was young
not hearing as much as feeling

not wanting to stir
and there's that photograph of Feldman

so ordinary-looking
with his horn-rimmed glasses

and his lumpy suit and perpetual cigarette
Ten thousand hours of practice, the book says

is what it takes to become an accomplished musician
I keep a log, practice daily

with a goal: 30 hours a week 1500 hours
a year 6 or 7 years let's say 10 just to be safe

I'm on my own, instruction sheets and fake books and stuff
It's not the Julliard or anything

Resolution, concentration, trying to make up all that time
getting 8 hours in some days. Just like having a job

When I think about it, ten thousand hours
five years in the service of the company

was what I'd signed up for with the railway
all those years ago.

Zombie

As nicknames go, it wasn't much
but it was better than Fat

and since there was no point fighting
he decided to make the best of it, acting cool

aloof, non-communicative. He practiced a stare,
never blinking until the other person

looked away. No one ever knew, for sure,
what he was thinking.

Otherwise, he seemed fairly normal, smart.
He developed a reputation for deep insight,

for profound observations. All he had to do
was talk less than the others. Still, he didn't like the nickname.

This was just before rock 'n roll
burst on the scene and kids would gather

at the neighbourhood parks
in the summer, hanging out, smoking.

It was boys and girls together, innocent stuff,
but just trying to get a handle on what it all meant.

Like I said, it was before rock, before Elvis,
but the kids still liked to sing

and there was this group, Somethin' Smith and the Redheads
who had a hit called, well, *Redhead*

and they had updated a couple of old tunes, *It's Only a Shanty*
in Old Shanty Town and *It's a Sin to Tell A Lie.*

Sin was on the charts then and some of the kids, sitting in the gloom of the tiny park building, wanted to sing it.

There were a couple of girls there
and that helped get things going. They sang

Be sure it's true when you say I love you,
It's a sin to tell a lie

and things went along pretty well
with the girls swaying, keeping time

and when they got to the part where the segue came,
Zombie stepped right in, he had it down cold and he sang

Cross my heart and I hope to die,
I'll never, never, never tell another white lie,

Took a little doll out on a date last night,
Next to her Gravel Gertie would have looked all right.

Now I'm between the devil and the deep-blue sea,
'Cause I said "Baby, you look good to me."

I told her I loved her but oh how I lied,
And now she's getting set to be my blushing bride.

If she leads me to the altar, I'm sunk,
'Cause I can't tell the preacher I was drunk.

So, Lord have mercy on a no account sinner,
Give me one more chance and let another guy win her,

Cross my heart and I hope to die,
I'll never, never, never tell another white lie.

They had all watched him, mesmerized. He had been careful
to keep the phrasing, the timing, exactly right.

They finished the song and everybody drifted away
and went home. The next day he came to the park

and stared straight ahead and didn't mention the song.
No one mentioned it.

Cello

After I'd learned the guitar
I wanted to buy a cello.

My wife wouldn't hear of it
said the cello made all music

sound like a dirge.
You don't want to play the bloody cello!

and that was that.
I consoled myself by listening

to Rostropovich and Yo-Yo Mah
and practising

12-bar blues chord progressions
in the basement.

I probably wouldn't have made
much of a cellist anyway,

given my age and late start, but
what about Ned Beatty

playing the cello
on *Homicide: Life on the Street*

accompanied by a beautiful young violinist
to boot? Okay, a real cellist

taught him how to fake the moves
but I believed it anyway, Ned was so

exuberant, so proud. Anything is possible
on television or in the movies

Robert Taylor played the cello in real life
before he ever became an actor. In fact,

he followed his teacher to California
and was discovered

by a talent scout
in the best Hollywood tradition.

I had never thought of Robert Taylor,
the movie star, as a real person

until I read that footnote, long after
he was dead, about him playing the cello.

It was like realizing Paul Newman
stayed married to the same woman

for fifty years
and sold salad dressing

and was five foot
eight inches tall

or that Boris Karloff's lisp was real,
that he dropped out of school,

worked (appropriately)
as a ditch-digger

before getting into acting
and organized a benefit in Regina

after the 1912 cyclone, standing,
for all his monstrous stature,

only five foot nine. Robert Taylor
was almost six feet tall

but one has to sit
to play the cello.

Breathing Some Life into the Doctor's Waiting Room

(For Bob Currie)

Come on, man, we can do it
I mean, we probably *look*
like a couple of old guys from some 60's band.
Think about it,

the place stifling hot, half the patients
probably with bubonic plague
or at least sounding like it, everyone
nervous, eyes shifting
from face to face
the showdown scene from
The Good, The Bad and The Ugly

and we stomp in, carrying our cases,
reach down   *click-click*   *click-click*
pull these two old battered dreadnaughts
up onto our knees
jeans and flannel shirts
two-day's growth of stubble
(well, a full beard for you)
and launch right into

Out on the Weekend

hitting those sweet, high
fifth and seventh fret voicings
A   Bm7   D

Then, before anyone can speak
we hit 'em with some C.C. Revival,
Stones, Troggs, you name it,

entire careers built on three-chord progressions.
We lay Sally down,
sing about how *Wonderful*
she is Tonight, chill out
with The Beatles, the haunting,
hardly-ever played
Things We Said Today

straightforward and tricky
and ending together, on cue,
banging down on that
shuddering, spooky E chord that ends
A Day in the Life

and as the chord rings
through every room
in every building in every town there ever was
echoing magically
for that endless moment,
we bend
return the guitars
to their shabby cases
snap them shut   *click-click*   *click-click*
stroll to the door
guitar cases in hand
and turn

daring anyone to draw…

Elvis Agonistes

I wish it were his profile
or his singing voice

or that endearing snarl
that we have in common

but it's our colons;
meandering through our lives

like the Mississippi or North Saskatchewan,
so drawn out and distended gastroenterologists

shake their heads in disbelief saying, sorry,
they just can't get past that certain point.

I've had nothing to eat but broth and jello
for the past eight days for all the good

that did. Our doctors sign slips
for barium x-rays

and we groan,
having been through all that before.

At the hospital, x-ray technicians
strap us to rotating tables

turn us this way and that, flip us
like pancakes, even stand us on our heads

pump in so much barium it drops from
the 14th most abundant element on earth

to the 16th. The technicians sweat, telling us
not to breathe as they take x-ray after x-ray,

their faces transparent
with concern and dismay.

Finally, they admit defeat and release
all that barium, much to our relief.

We sit together in skimpy white gowns
waiting for our results

and he says, in a voice that sounds exactly
the way you'd think it would sound,

I'd surely appreciate it if you wouldn't mention
seeing me here.

The nurse pokes her head in,
telling us we can get dressed.

He stands in front of the mirror,
combing back that long black hair and I notice

he wears his collar up
just like in his photographs.

I never imagined
this would be the way we'd meet

and I want to tell him
about singing *Heartbreak Hotel*

in that empty tank car
all those years ago

as he smiles and waves goodbye
and slips out the back door.

Of His Demise

Glenn Gould died Saturday night
on the dance floor of the Senior Centre

I mean Glenn *Cannonball* Gould, the mailman
not the eccentric pianist

the guy who played baseball and basketball around the city
which would explain how the Times-Herald

would have had his photograph
in its archives. Can you imagine

the shock he had
opening his paper that October day in 1982?

and if it's true that people
get the kind of newspaper they deserve

some of those people
will be scratching their heads, saying

I thought he died years ago, but they'd be wrong
because he went on living another 28 years

Oh, I'm sure
he died years ago, they'll say

and be wrong because he died right there
on the dance floor Saturday night

and down in the dark composing room
the lay-out man is centering that famous photograph of him

on the kitchen chair with the sawed-off legs
hunched over the piano

his ear right down at the keyboard, oblivious
to all but the music

Skye Staircase

my grandfather came from Skye
the Isle just off Scotland's wild
rough-shingled shores
and he loved the *Skye Boat Song*

Fly, bonny boat
Like a bird on the wing
Onward the sailors cry

I remember him best
after he retired to Vancouver
a slim shadowy figure
bent over his cluttered workbench
in that cool shadowy grotto the structure
a garage in name only
never having housed a car
at least not in my memory
where he sucked his pipe
and built furniture in solitude
or tended to his compost pile
at the back fence

I sing for him now the *Skye Boat Song*
loud and recklessly, fiercely defiant
against the English
in return for his help
in building my oak staircase

I ask him for his help
and me a grandfather myself
and it seems to me now
he was waiting all this time
for me to call.

Fly, bonny boat
Like a bird on the wing
Onward the sailors cry
Carry the lad who was born to be king
Over the sea to Skye

Elvis Presley's 80th Birthday (January 8, 2015)

will be more exploited
than celebrated like
everything else in his life
from the moment of that first
Sun recording and I was thinking
how easy it must have been
for him to leave it all behind
and end up alive and well
and living in (fill in the blank)
all these years, all of us
looking for someone in a
rhinestone-studded white suit
and a cape for Christ's sake.

I wish him a good one, a cake
with grandchildren crowding around
and no one asking him to break into song
on some pastel sound stage
no cameras or microphones,
no National Enquirer reporters
or whatever they're called,
birthday wrapping paper
strewn around the floor, the sink
piled high with dishes
and that sweet moment of silence
when everyone's finally gone home.

Dancer

She's intelligent, accomplished, a force
among her contemporaries, even a bit

intimidating at times but she can't dance.
She's tried, letting men drag her across the floor

until the music stopped and they could escape
but she needs to dance, needs to be *danced*

and she sees him on the floor, smooth, confident,
decides he will be her partner.

He leads her onto the floor, knows enough
not to try to teach her to dance, just dances,

enveloping her so that it's easy, so that she has
no choice but to follow, no place to look

but in his eyes. Has she become so light
her feet barely touch the floor or is he so strong

that he can be gentle in every move? People
are watching them, watching the couple

on the floor and she knows
they must be watching him but he makes it seem

they're watching a couple. He is doing what no man
has ever been able to do and he's making it seem

so natural. Her mind begins to analyze and she stops it.
He moves instinctively and that's what she wants now.

She tries to relax and move with him and when
the music stops she refuses to leave the floor, waits

for the next song. It's a waltz and he sings as they dance.
She loves that.

She knows him, knows who he is, knows his name
but she says;

Who are you? Where did you come from? She knows
she's never going home.

Garden

In summer, I make my own
liquid fertilizer, a gunny sack

of compost, rotting for the past
three years, leaves,

grass cuttings, cow
manure submerged

in a barrel of water left open
to the summer sun. It's putrid,

it stinks, but that's what you want,
pure organic juice

to feed the flowers and tomatoes,
cucumbers swarming over the trellis

beans, carrots, potatoes everything enormous.
I feed it back into the lawns, nature,

an unapologetic cannibal. I dip
my bucket, swilling the garden,

remembering the daily ritual
of throwing the slop pail into the alley.

Why didn't we think, back then,
of nurturing the garden instead

of wasting good fertilizer down the ruts,
into the gravel and dust of the street?

My granddaughter won't go near the barrel.
I assure her that, except for the cow manure,

we could drink it, like soup. She doesn't buy that
but she'll eat the sweet

tart tomatoes, the creamy cucumbers
(there's no other adjective

to describe them)
and grow blossom and mature,

becoming even more beautiful
no perfect day like this anywhere else

cool breeze under that bright warm sun
the enormous calm silence

the smell of new-mown grass, enough
to make you forgive winter

and the trenches of Saskatchewan politics
enough to make you stay, hoping

for one more day like this
for all our time to come my memory is you

shading your eyes the wind in your hair
this day is your gift to me

anything I give you lost
in your light

Acknowledgements

The author wishes to acknowledge the invaluable support of the Poets Combine, and to thank Byrna Barclay, Robert Currie, Judith Krause, Katherine Lawrence, Bruce Rice and Paul Wilson for their help and criticism and his editor, Harold Rhenisch, whose vision, dedication and hard work made this book so much better.

My thanks also, to the staff and board at Coteau Books, to Nik Burton, who accepted my manuscript for publication and Susan Buck for her assistance in design and editing, and to the Saskatchewan Writers Guild, so important to writers.

About the Author

JIM McLEAN had a long career with Canadian Pacific Railway and with Transport Canada, living and working in various Canadian locations. He is an original member of the Moose Jaw Movement poetry group, and his work has appeared in magazines and anthologies and on CBC Radio. He is the author of *The Secret Life of Railroaders* and co-author of *Wildflowers Across the Prairies*. His illustrations have appeared on book covers and in several literary and scientific publications. He currently lives in Moose Jaw, Saskatchewan.